MY FIRST
BAKING
B·O·O·K

HELEN DREW

ALFRED A. KNOPF 🐎 NEW YORK

For James Magee

A Dorling Kindersley Book

Design Mathewson Bull
Photography Dave King
Home Economist Jane Suthering
Series Editor Angela Wilkes
Art Director Roger Priddy

THIS IS A BORZOI BOOK PUBLISHED BY ALFRED A KNOPF, INC.

First American edition, 1991

2 4 6 8 10 9 7 5 3 1

Library of Congress Cataloging-in-Publication Data

Drew, Helen
   My first baking book / Helen Drew : [illustrations by Brian Delf].
      p.   cm.
   "A Dorling Kindersley book" — T.p. verso.
   Summary: Step-by-step photographs and instructions show readers
how to make the snacks and desserts everyone likes.
   ISBN 0-679-81545-7 (trade) — ISBN 0-679-91545-1 (lib. bdg.)
   1. Cake—Juvenile literature. 2. Baking—Juvenile literature.
[1. Cake. 2. Baking. 3. Cookery.]   I. Delf, Brian, ill.
II. Title.
TX771.D74 1991
641.B'65—dc20   91-10239

Phototypeset by The Setting Studio, Newcastle
Color reproduction by Colourscan, Singapore
Printed and bound in Italy by L.E.G.O.

Dorling Kindersley would like to thank Jonathan Buckley,
Phoebe Thoms, Meg Jansz and Mandy Earey for their
help in producing this book.

Illustrations by Brian Delf

CONTENTS

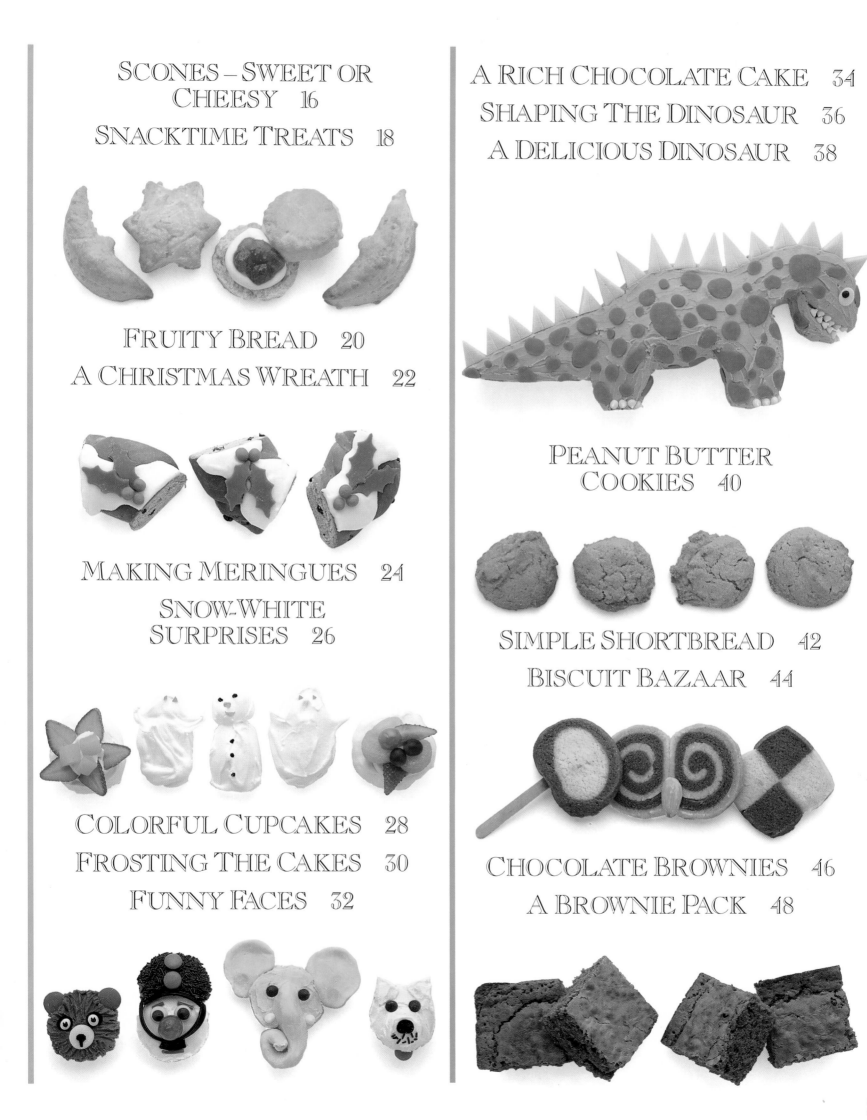

BAKING BY PICTURES

My First Baking Book shows you how to bake lots of delicious cakes and cookies. Each colorful recipe shows all the ingredients you will need – life-size! Step-by-step photographs and clear instructions tell you what to do, and at the end of each recipe are some great ideas for decorations. Below are the things to look for in each recipe, and on the next page is a list of important cook's rules for you to read before you start baking.

How to use this book

How many cakes?
Each recipe tells you how many things the ingredients make. To make more, double or triple the quantities shown.

The ingredients
All the ingredients you need for each recipe are shown life-size so that you can see if you have the right amounts.

Cook's tools
These illustrated checklists show you all the cooking utensils you will need to have ready before you start baking.

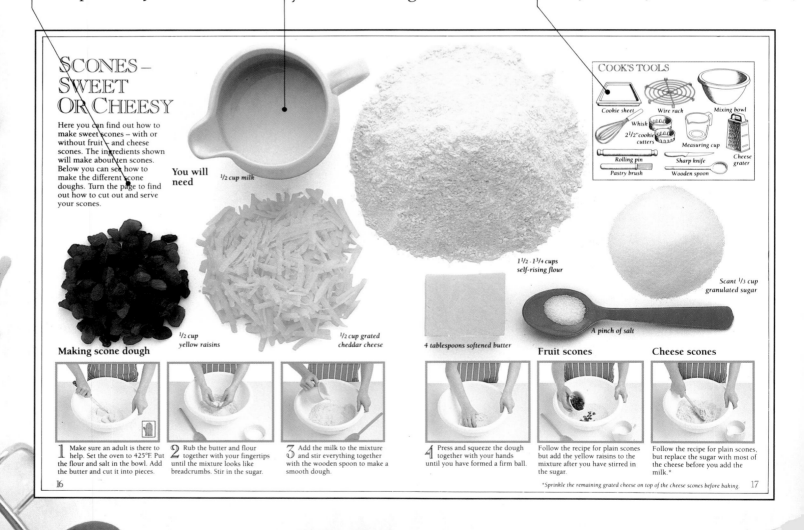

SCONES – SWEET OR CHEESY

Here you can find out how to make sweet scones – with or without fruit – and cheese scones. The ingredients shown will make about ten scones. Below you can see how to make the different scone doughs. Turn the page to find out how to cut out and serve your scones.

You will need

½ cup milk

COOK'S TOOLS
Cookie sheet   Wire rack   Mixing bowl
Whisk
2½" cookie cutters   Measuring cup
Rolling pin   Sharp knife   Cheese grater
Pastry brush   Wooden spoon

½ cup yellow raisins

½ cup grated cheddar cheese

1½ - 1¾ cups self-rising flour

Scant ⅓ cup granulated sugar

4 tablespoons softened butter

A pinch of salt

Making scone dough

1 Make sure an adult is there to help. Set the oven to 425°F. Put the flour and salt in the bowl. Add the butter and cut it into pieces.

2 Rub the butter and flour together with your fingertips until the mixture looks like breadcrumbs. Stir in the sugar.

3 Add the milk to the mixture and stir everything together with the wooden spoon to make a smooth dough.

4 Press and squeeze the dough together with your hands until you have formed a firm ball.

Fruit scones
Follow the recipe for plain scones but add the yellow raisins to the mixture after you have stirred in the sugar.

Cheese scones
Follow the recipe for plain scones, but replace the sugar with most of the cheese before you add the milk.*

*Sprinkle the remaining grated cheese on top of the cheese scones before baking.

16   17

4

Cook's rules

1 Only bake when an adult is there to help you.

2 Make sure you have everything you need before you start to bake.

3 Always wash your hands and wear an apron and roll up your sleeves before you start.

4 Wear oven mitts when touching hot things and when putting things in the oven or taking them out.

5 If you get burned: Hold the burn under cold running water immediately and call for help.

6 Turn saucepan handles to the side of the stove so you do not bump into them.

7 Never leave the kitchen when gas or electric range is turned on.

8 Always turn the oven off after you have finished baking.

Step-by-step
Step-by-step photographs and easy-to-follow instructions show you what to do at each stage of the recipe.

The oven mitt symbol
Whenever you see this symbol in a recipe, always put on oven mitts and ask an adult to help you.

The finished result
The picture at the end of each recipe shows the baked and decorated cakes and cookies life-size.

SNACKTIME TREATS

You can make scones in lots of shapes and sizes. Use different-shaped cookie cutters to make small scones, or make a big scone round with your hands. All scones taste best when they are still warm, either on their own or with butter. For a really special treat, try filling plain or fruit scones with jam and whipped cream.

COOK'S TOOLS

Small bowl
Whisk or eggbeater
Sharp knife
Knife

You will need

Jam

½ cup heavy cream

PLAIN SCONES

Strawberry jam

Whipped cream

CHEESE SCONES

Cutting out the scones

1 Grease a cookie sheet. Gently roll out the dough until it is ¾ inch thick. Cut out shapes with cookie cutters dipped in flour.

2 Put the scones on a cookie sheet* and brush them with milk. Bake them for 12 to 15 minutes, until risen. Cool them on a wire rack.

A scone round

Whipping the cream

Flatten the dough into a circle 1 inch thick. Score the top into eight wedges,** then brush it with milk. Bake for about 25 minutes.

Using the eggbeater, beat the cream in the bowl until it is thick.† Cut the plain or fruit scones in half and top with jam and cream.*

A FRUIT SCONE ROUND

Grated cheddar cheese sprinkled on before baking

18   *Sprinkle the remaining grated cheese on top of the cheese scones before baking.

**Ask an adult to help you with any cutting.   †With an adult's help, a handmixer may be used instead.   19

PUFF PASTRY

You can make lots of mouth-watering pastries with ready-made puff pastry. Here you can find out how to make currant-filled Eccles cakes, palmiers (palm tree-shaped pastries) and cheese twists.

The ingredients shown are enough to make about thirty pastries. Turn the page to see the finished results.

You will need

1 egg

¹/3 cup
light brown sugar, packed
(for palmiers)

¹/2 teaspoon white granulated
sugar (for Eccles cakes)

¹/4 teaspoon ground nutmeg
(for Eccles cakes)

1 tablespoon
softened butter
(for Eccles cakes)

12 oz ready-made puff pastry

COOK'S TOOLS

Measuring cup   Cookie sheet   Small bowl

4-inch plain cookie cutters   Wire rack

Rolling pin

Wooden spoon   Fork

Sharp knife   Pastry brush

Spatula (not shown)
Cup (not shown)

6

1 tablespoon light brown sugar, packed
(for Eccles cakes)

Heaping tablespoon candied
citrus peel (for Eccles cakes)

1/3 cup chopped roasted hazelnuts or filberts (for palmiers)

1/2 cup grated cheddar cheese (for cheese twists)

1/3 cup currants or raisins (for Eccles cakes)

What to do

1 Set the oven to 425°F.* Grease a cookie sheet with some butter. Beat the egg in a cup with a fork.

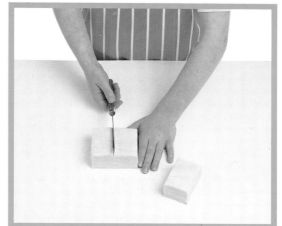

2 Put the pastry on a floured surface and divide it into three equal pieces. You will need one piece of pastry for each recipe.

Eccles cakes

1 Roll out the pastry on a floured surface until it is 1/8 inch thick. Cut out six circles with the plain cookie cutter.

2 Put the currants, peel, butter, tablespoon light brown sugar and nutmeg in a small bowl and mix them together.

3 Put a teaspoon of mixture in the center of each circle. Brush the circles with egg and pinch the edges together.

4 Turn the bundles over and press them flat. Cut two slits in the top. Brush them with egg and sprinkle white sugar on top.

*Ask an adult to help you.

Pastries on Parade

Hazelnut palmiers

1 Roll out the pastry into a rectangle 12 inches by 8 inches. Brush it with egg and sprinkle on two thirds of the sugar and nuts.

2 Fold the short sides of the rectangle into the middle. Brush them with egg and sprinkle with the rest of the sugar and nuts.

3 Fold the folded edges into the middle. Brush the top with egg. Fold the pastry in half to form a roll. Cut it into 16 slices.*

Cheese twists

1 Roll out the pastry into a rectangle 10 inches by 8 inches. Brush it with egg. Sprinkle the cheese over half of the rectangle.

2 Fold the pastry over the cheese to make a sandwich and roll it flat. Trim the edges with a knife.* Brush the sandwich with egg.

3 Cut the sandwich lengthwise into 20 strips.* Twist each strip several times and press the ends onto the baking tray.

Baking the pastries

Make sure an adult is there to help. Bake the pastries on a greased cookie sheet. Cheese twists and palmiers should be baked for 10 minutes and the Eccles cakes for 15 minutes. The pastries are ready when they are crisp and golden brown. Once they are baked, take them out of the oven and use a spatula to put them on a wire rack to cool.

Pastries taste best on the day they are made. You can eat them as soon as they are cool!

8

*Ask an adult to help you with any cutting.

The finished pastries

ECCLES CAKES

HAZELNUT PALMIERS

CHEESE TWISTS

9

PASTRY IN A PAN

Choux pastry* is great fun to make, since it puffs up to two or three times its size when you bake it. Here and on the next five pages you can find out how to make and decorate lots of different choux cakes. The ingredients shown will make about five each of the spiders, puffs, snakes and éclairs, and lots of worms.

You will need

7 tablespoons butter

³/4 teaspoon salt

1 scant cup white flour

4 eggs

1 egg, slightly beaten

1 cup water

COOK'S TOOLS

Wooden board   Small bowl   Strainer   Saucepan   Measuring cup

Cookie sheet   Pastry bag with ¹/8", ¹/4", ³/8", and ¹/2" plain nozzles   Wire rack   Toothpicks

Fork   Pastry brush   Wooden spoon

*Choux is French for "puff."

What to do

1 Make sure an adult is there to help. Set the oven to 400°F. Grease the cookie sheet. Sift the flour into the small bowl.

2 Put the water, salt and butter into the pan and heat them gently until the butter has melted and the mixture begins to bubble.

3 Remove the saucepan from the heat and place it on a wooden board. Add all the flour to the mixture at once.

4 Beat the batter vigorously until it comes away from the sides of the saucepan. Leave it to cool for one or two minutes.

5 Beat the four eggs in the small bowl. Add them to the batter a little at a time until it is smooth and shiny.

6 Fit a nozzle* into the pastry bag. Put the bag in the measuring cup and fold its top over the sides. Spoon in the batter.

7 When the bag is full, twist the top to close it. To start piping, squeeze the pastry down through the nozzle.

8 Pipe your shapes onto the greased cookie sheet and brush them with beaten egg. Bake them for 20 to 25 minutes, until golden.

9 Remove the shapes from the oven and when cool enough to touch, prick each one once with a toothpick, and leave to cool further.

Turn the page to see which nozzle to use to pipe each shape.

11

LIGHT AS AIR

You can pipe choux pastry into any shape you like. Follow the instructions at the bottom of the page to make spiders, snakes, worms, puffs and éclairs. When the shapes are cool, fill them with whipped cream and top them with the chocolate icing shown opposite.

You will need

4 oz semisweet chocolate

³/4 cup confectioners' sugar

PUFFS

To make puffs and spiders' bodies, use the ¹/2-inch nozzle and pipe small mounds onto the cookie sheet.

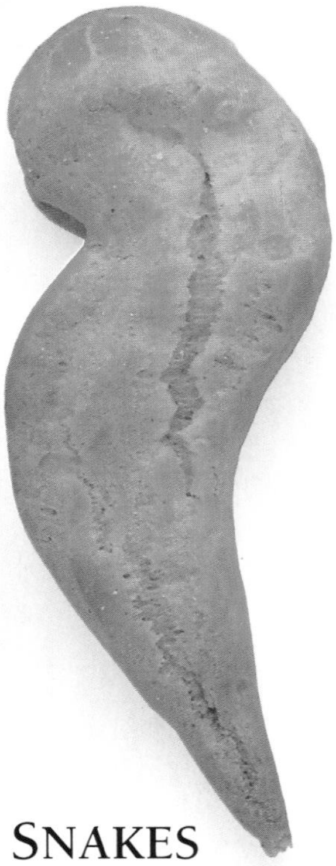

SNAKES

Use the ³/8-inch nozzle to make the snakes. Start at the head of the snake and pipe a wiggly line for its body.

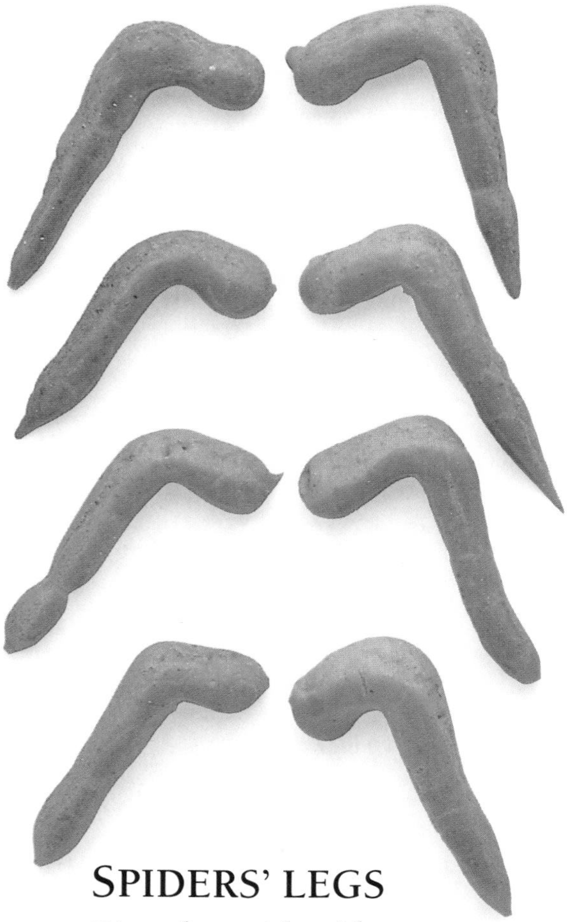

SPIDERS' LEGS

Pipe the spiders' legs using the ¹/8-inch nozzle. Make four left legs and four right legs for each spider.

WORMS

These are piped with a ¹/4-inch nozzle. Pipe the worms as though you are writing commas

2 tablespoons butter

3 tablespoons water

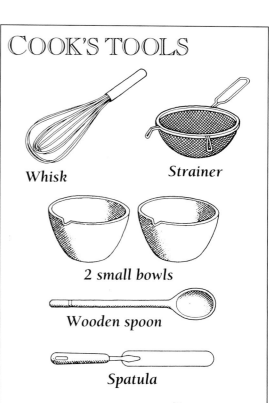

1 cup heavy cream

What to do

1 Whip the cream† in a small bowl until it is thick and fluffy. Slice the puffs and éclairs in half and spoon the cream into them.*

2 Cut the butter and chocolate into pieces.* Put them in the saucepan and stir them together over a low heat until they melt.

3 Stir in the water. Remove the mixture from the heat. Sift the confectioners' sugar and add it to the mixture. Stir until smooth.

4 Spread icing along the buns, éclairs and snakes with a spatula. Dip the worms in the icing with your fingers.

ECLAIRS

Eclairs are made with the 1/2-inch nozzle. Pipe 2-inch lines of pastry for mini-éclairs and 4-inch lines for big ones.

†Add sugar to taste, if desired.   *Ask an adult to help you with any cutting.

CHOUX SHOW

Here are some ideas for decorating your choux shapes. The spider's web was made by piping some of the chocolate icing onto a large white plate. Try piping other animals to make a choux zoo for a special occasion or party.

The finished cakes

Raisins

Red licorice

Rainbow sprinkles

Rainbow shots

SNAKES

The snakes are filled with cre⟨am⟩ and topped with chocolate icin⟨g⟩. Use dabs of cream and raisin pieces for eyes and red licorice for a tongue.

Raisin-and-cream eyes

Red licorice forked tongue

Rainbow shot markings

SPIDERS

To make spiders, cut some puffs in half and fill each half with cream. Arrange four legs on each side of the spiders and pipe more cream on top. Add pieces of raisin for eyes.

WORMS

The worms have been dipped in chocolate icing and then covered in rainbow sprinkles before the icing set.

Rainbow sprinkles

ECLAIRS

Chocolate éclairs are topped with a thick layer of the chocolate icing and filled with lots of cream filling.

PUFFS AND PROFITEROLES

Choux puffs can be eaten as individual cakes as shown here, or as one big dessert, filled with cream and covered with lots of chocolate icing.

15

SCONES – SWEET OR CHEESY

Here you can find out how to make sweet scones – with or without fruit – and cheese scones. The ingredients shown will make about ten scones. Below you can see how to make the different scone doughs. Turn the page to find out how to cut out and serve your scones.

You will need

1/2 cup milk

1/2 cup yellow raisins

1/2 cup grated cheddar cheese

Making scone dough

1 Make sure an adult is there to help. Set the oven to 425°F. Put the flour and salt in the bowl. Add the butter and cut it into pieces.

2 Rub the butter and flour together with your fingertips until the mixture looks like breadcrumbs. Stir in the sugar.

3 Add the milk to the mixture and stir everything together with the wooden spoon to make a smooth dough.

COOK'S TOOLS

Cookie sheet · Wire rack · Mixing bowl
Whisk
2¹/₂" cookie cutters · Measuring cup
Rolling pin · Sharp knife · Cheese grater
Pastry brush · Wooden spoon

1¹/₂ - 1³/₄ cups self-rising flour

Scant ¹/₃ cup granulated sugar

A pinch of salt

4 tablespoons softened butter

Fruit scones

Cheese scones

4 Press and squeeze the dough together with your hands until you have formed a firm ball.

Follow the recipe for plain scones but add the yellow raisins to the mixture after you have stirred in the sugar.

Follow the recipe for plain scones, but replace the sugar with most of the cheese before you add the milk.*

*Sprinkle the remaining grated cheese on top of the cheese scones before baking.

Snacktime Treats

You can make scones in lots of shapes and sizes. Use different-shaped cookie cutters to make small scones, or make a big scone round with your hands. All scones taste best when they are still warm, either on their own or with butter. For a really special treat, try filling plain or fruit scones with jam and whipped cream.

Cook's Tools

Small bowl

Whisk or eggbeater

Sharp knife

Knife

Jam

Cutting out the scones

1 Grease a cookie sheet. Gently roll out the dough until it is 3/4 inch thick. Cut out shapes with cookie cutters dipped in flour.

2 Put the scones on a cookie sheet* and brush them with milk. Bake them for 12 to 15 minutes, until risen. Cool them on a wire rack.

A scone round

Whipping the cream

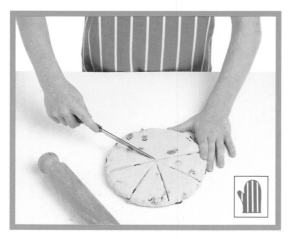

Flatten the dough into a circle 1 inch thick. Score the top into eight wedges,** then brush it with milk. Bake for about 25 minutes.

Using the eggbeater, beat the cream in the bowl until it is thick.† Cut the plain or fruit scones in half and top with jam and cream.**

Sprinkle the remaining grated cheese on top of the cheese scones before baking.

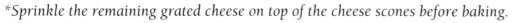

*1/2 cup
heavy cream*

PLAIN SCONES

*Strawberry
jam*

Whipped cream

CHEESE SCONES

**A FRUIT
SCONE ROUND**

*Grated cheddar cheese
sprinkled on before baking*

**Ask an adult to help you with any cutting.

†With an adult's help, a handmixer may be used instead.

FRUITY BREAD

A Christmas wreath that not only tastes good, it looks very festive too! Here you can see all you need to make a fruity bread wreath. The wreath will rise more quickly if you put it in an oiled plastic bag and then leave it in a warm place. Turn the page to see how to make the icing and marzipan decoration for your wreath.

3 fl oz warm milk, heated to body temperature

You will need

2 tablespoons butter

1 egg

1/2 teaspoon salt

1/4 cup light brown sugar, packed

1 1/4 cups flour

What to do

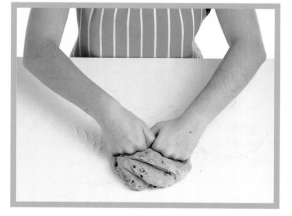

1 Ask an adult to help. Set oven to 400°F. Put the sugar, flour, yeast, salt, spices and cinnamon in the bowl and stir them together.

2 Add the butter and cut it up.* Rub everything together with your fingertips until the mixture looks like fine breadcrumbs.

3 Add the fruit, egg and milk. Mix them together to make a ball of dough. Knead the dough on a floured surface for five minutes.

20

Ask an adult to help you with any cutting.

1 packet yeast

Heaping tablespoon candied citrus peel

1 teaspoon ground cinnamon

¹/₂ teaspoon ground mixed spices (combine equal parts nutmeg, allspice, cinnamon and cloves)

¹/₃ cup raisins

4 Roll the dough into two sausages about 24 inches long. Put the sausages side by side and twist them together.

5 Bend the twist into a ring on the cookie sheet. Wet the ends of the twist with water and stick them together.

6 Leave the ring in a warm place until it has doubled in size.† Bake it for 20 to 25 minutes, then move it onto a wire rack to cool.

†This takes about 1 hour. 21

A Christmas Wreath

Turn your fruity ring into a Christmas treat with a tangy lemon icing and some marzipan leaves and berries. You can find out how to make marzipan on page 37, but if you prefer, you can use ready-made marzipan or prepared fondant icing.*

You will need

1 heaping tablespoon marzipan (for holly leaves)

3/4 tablespoon marzipan (for holly berries)

1 tablespoon lemon juice mixed with 1 tablespoon water

12 drops green food coloring

12 drops red food coloring

Scant 1 1/2 cups confectioners' sugar

Coloring marzipan

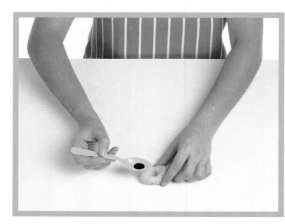

Make a hole with your finger in the marzipan and add the food coloring. Mix the marzipan until it is an even color.

Holly leaves

Roll the green marzipan out on a surface dusted with confectioners' sugar until it is 1/8 inch thick. Cut out 12 leaves with the cutter.

Holly berries

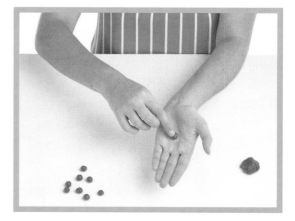

Take small pieces of red marzipan and roll them into balls with your fingers. Try to keep all the balls the same size. Makes 15 to 20.

*Prepared fondant may be ordered from Maid of Scandinavia, 32-44 Raleigh Avenue, Minneapolis, MN 55416. Phone 800-328-6722.

Making icing

1 Sift the sugar into the small bowl. Add the lemon juice and stir with the wooden spoon until the icing is smooth.

2 Spoon the icing along the top of the wreath and let it drip down the sides. Decorate the wreath before the icing sets.

The finished Christmas wreath

Marzipan holly leaves

Snowy white icing

Marzipan holly berries

*Cut the ring into wedges and serve with some berries and leaves on each wedge.** *

†Use a knife if you can't find any cutters.

**Ask an adult to help you with any cutting.

MAKING MERINGUES

Meringues are deliciously sweet and crunchy and are made from only the whites of eggs, some sugar and a little salt. Separating the egg white from the yolk is quite tricky because yolks break very easily, so always start with more eggs than you need! Be very careful not to allow any yolk to mix with the egg whites, or the recipe won't work.

Meringues take two hours to cook because they have to be baked at a low temperature to keep them white. Start baking in the morning, so that you don't have to stay up all night!

COOK'S TOOLS

Cookie sheet

Small pitcher

Cup

Mixing bowl

Baking parchment

Teaspoon

Spatula

Tablespoon

Whisk or eggbeater

Small bowl

Sharp knife

Scissors

You will need

A pinch of salt

2 eggs

Candied cherries

Raisins

1/2 cup granulated sugar

Candied orange peel

24

What to do

1 Ask an adult to help you. Set the oven at 225°F. Cover the cookie sheet with baking parchment or aluminum foil.

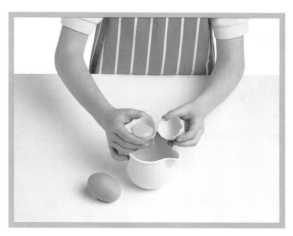

2 *Crack one egg in half and pour the yolk from one half of the shell into the other, letting the egg white fall into the pitcher.

3 Empty the yolk into the cup and the white into the small bowl. Do the same thing again to separate the second egg.

4 Add a pinch of salt to the egg whites in the small bowl. Beat the egg whites with the eggbeater until they form stiff peaks.†

5 Beat the sugar into the egg whites a little at a time, until you have used all the sugar and the meringue looks glossy.

Nests

Shape a heaping tablespoonful of meringue into a mound on a cookie sheet. Make a hollow in the middle with a spoon.

Ghosts

Spread heaping tablespoonfuls of meringue into ghost shapes with a teaspoon. Cut pieces of candied cherry to make eyes.

Snowmen

Use a teaspoonful of meringue for the head and a tablespoonful for the body. Decorate with pieces of raisin, candied peel and cherry.

6 Bake the meringue ghosts, snowmen and nests slowly for 2 to 2¼ hours until firm. Put them on a wire rack to cool.

*Ask an adult to help you with this.   †With an adult's help, a handmixer may be used instead.

SNOW-WHITE SURPRISES

Meringue nests make luscious desserts when
they are filled with cream and fruit. Use canned
fruit cocktail or pieces of fresh, soft fruit (like
the ones shown here) and arrange them in
pleasing designs on the cream-filled nests.

You could make nests at Easter, and fill them
with chocolate eggs, or make ghosts for a
Halloween treat. Snowmen are great fun as
Christmas decorations that you can eat!

*Canned, pitted
cherries*   *Canned mandarin orange segments*

You will need

¹/₂ cup heavy cream

Seedless red and green grapes

Strawberries

Canned peach chunks

Filling the nests

1 Pour the cream into a small
bowl. Add sugar to taste, if
desired. Beat the cream until it is
thick and forms soft peaks.†

2 Cut off all the strawberry tops.
Slice some of the strawberries
and cut others into quarters with a
sharp knife.*

3 Spoon the whipped cream into
the nests and arrange the
pieces of fruit in pretty designs on
top of them.

26   †*With an adult's help, a handmixer may be used.*

* *Ask an adult to help you.*

The finished meringues

MERINGUE NESTS

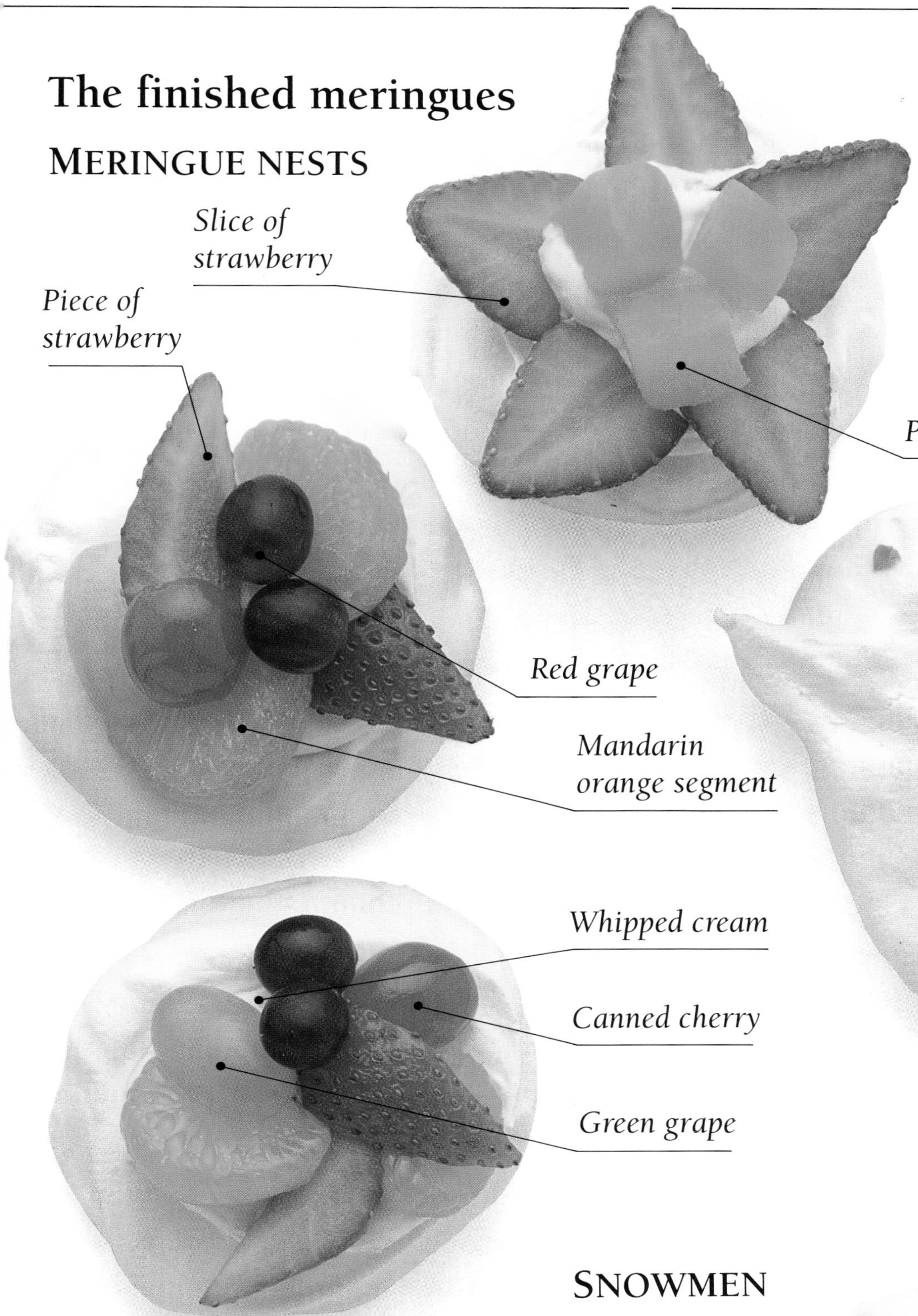

Slice of
strawberry

Piece of
strawberry

Red grape

Mandarin
orange segment

Whipped cream

Canned cherry

Green grape

GHOSTS

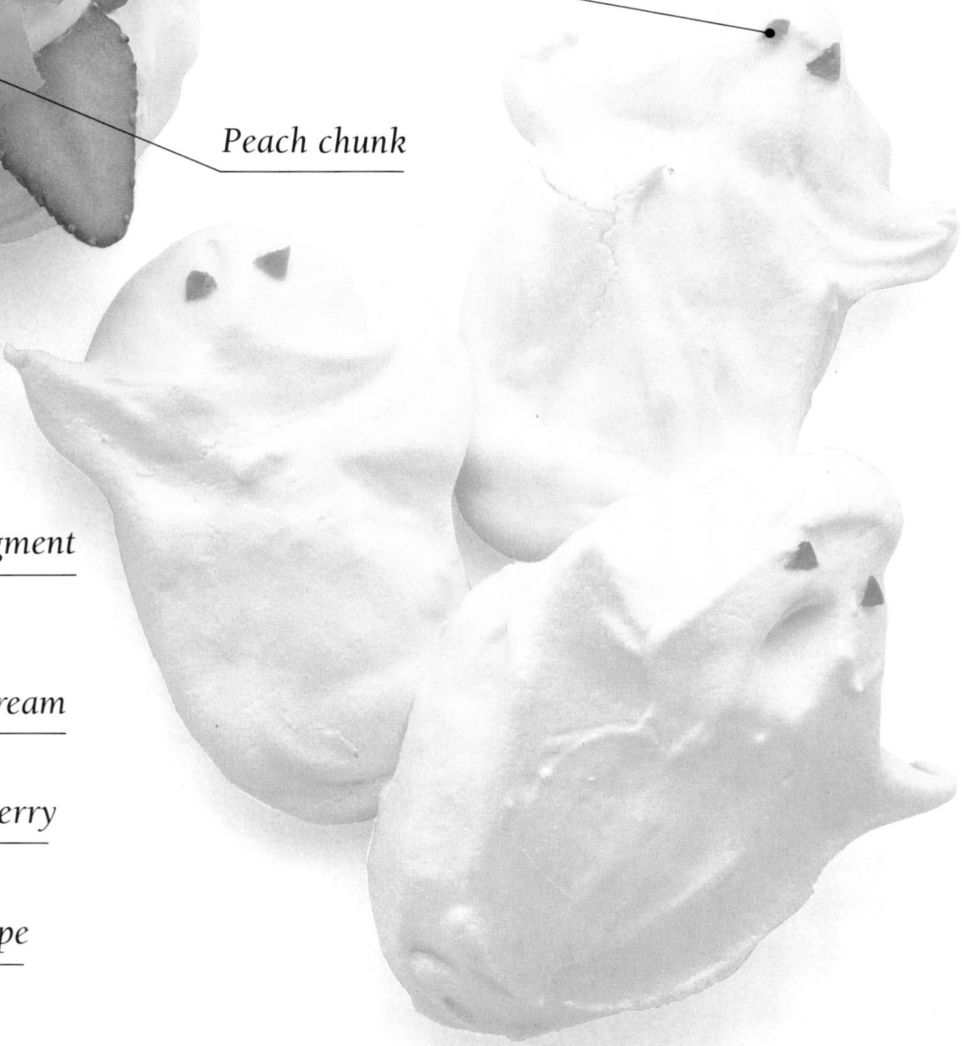

Pieces of candied
cherry for eyes

Peach chunk

SNOWMEN

Slice of candied cherry
for a mouth

Nose made from a
triangle of candied peel

Raisin eyes

Raisin buttons

COLORFUL CUPCAKES

Cupcakes are simple and quick to make. Here you can see everything you will need to make about ten regular and ten small plain or cherry cupcakes. If you wish to make more, you will have to double or triple the amounts of ingredients shown. Don't forget that you will need more frosting too!

On the next four pages there are lots of exciting ideas for frosting and decorating all your cupcakes.

You will need

2 eggs

6 candied cherries

1/2 cup (1 stick) softened margarine or butter

1/2 cup granulated sugar

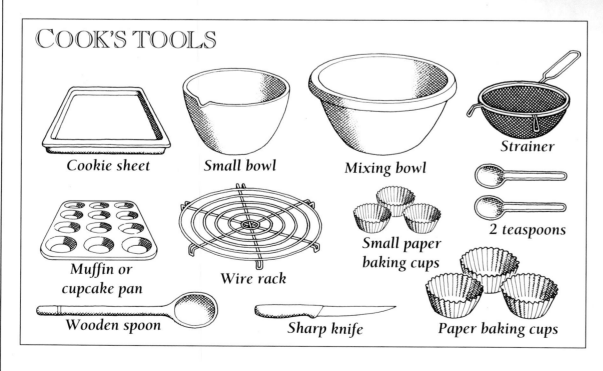

COOK'S TOOLS

Cookie sheet   *Small bowl*   *Mixing bowl*   *Strainer*

Muffin or cupcake pan   *Wire rack*   *Small paper baking cups*   *2 teaspoons*

Wooden spoon   *Sharp knife*   *Paper baking cups*

What to do

1 Ask an adult to help you. Set oven to 350°F. Put the larger baking cups in the muffin pan and the small cups on the cookie sheet.

2 Sift the self-rising flour into the mixing bowl. Add the margarine and the sugar to the flour.

3 Break the eggs into the bowl. Beat everything together with the wooden spoon until the batter is smooth and creamy.

4 To make cherry cupcakes, cut the candied cherries into small pieces with a sharp knife* and stir them into the cake mixture.

5 Put two teaspoonfuls of batter into each larger paper cup and one teaspoonful into each small one.

6 Bake the small cupcakes for 10 to 15 minutes and the regular ones for 20 to 25 minutes. †Then put them on a wire rack to cool.

3/4 cup self-rising flour

*Ask an adult to help you.

†When cool enough to touch.

FROSTING THE CAKES

You can make lots of different frostings for your cupcakes. Here you can find out how to make chocolate, white and pink buttercream frostings and how to color prepared fondant icing and mold it into shapes.* Look on the next two pages for decorating ideas.

You will need

¹/₂ cup (1 stick) very soft butter

*¹/₃ cup firmly packed ready-made fondant**

2 tablespoons cocoa powder

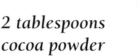

3 drops red food coloring

1¹/₂ - 1³/₄ cup confectioners' sugar

COOK'S TOOLS

Mixing bowl   2 small bowls

Wooden spoon

Sharp knife

Strainer   Knife

30

Ready-made fondant may be ordered from Maid of Scandinavia, 32-44 Raleigh Avenue, Minneapolis, MN 55416. Phone 800-328-6722.

What to do

1 Put half the butter into the mixing bowl and cut it into small pieces.* Beat it with the wooden spoon until it is creamy.

2 Sift ¾ cup of confectioners' sugar into a small bowl. Mix the sugar into the butter a little at a time until the frosting is creamy.†

3 Put half of the frosting into another small bowl and beat in the red coloring to make it pink. The other half is the white frosting.

Fondant icing

4 For chocolate frosting, use a scant ¾ cup confectioners' sugar and all the cocoa powder and follow steps 1 and 2 above.

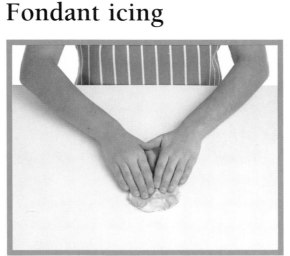

1 To make pink fondant icing, add 3 drops of red coloring to the fondant. Mix it until the color is even.

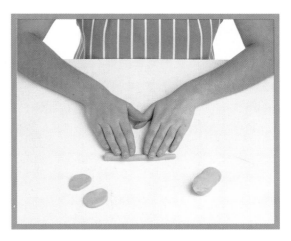

2 Make a roll of fondant for the elephant's trunk and shape flat circles for its ears. Make pig's ears from flat ovals of fondant.

Cakes with faces

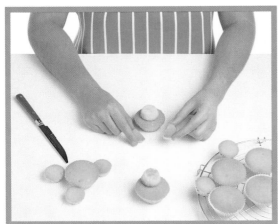

1 Take the paper cups off the cupcakes. Arrange the regular and small cupcakes together to make faces with ears or noses.

2 Frost the bottom and sides of a small cupcake and stick it on top of a regular cupcake covered with the same color icing.

3 When you have frosted all your cupcakes, give them faces by decorating them with candies before the frosting sets.

Ask an adult to help you.
†*A half teaspoon of vanilla or almond extract may be added for extra flavor.*

FUNNY FACES

There are lots of ways to decorate your cupcakes. You will need to look out for all sorts of candies to use for decoration. Copy the soldier, butterflies and animals shown here, or experiment with some ideas of your own.

Try making funny face cakes that look like your family and pets for a special family meal and use the cake faces as place cards at the table.

You will need

Licorice pieces

Red licorice string

Licorice strips

White chocolate chips

Chocolate chips

Candied cherries

White chocolate buttons

Chocolate buttons

Candy-covered chocolates

Chocolate sprinkles

CHERRY CUPCAKES

Eat your cherry cupcakes as they are, or frosted and decorated with candy.

Pieces of candied cherry

BUTTERFLIES

Cake wings

Buttercream frosting

Cut a circle out of some small cupcakes and then cut the circles in half to make wings. Fill the hole in the cupcakes with buttercream frosting and put a wing on each side.

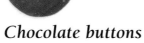

PIG

Chocolate chip eyes

Pink fondant ears

Chocolate chip nostrils

Red candy-covered chocolate tongue

SEAL

Chocolate chip and white chocolate button eyes

Licorice whiskers

SOLDIER

Chocolate sprinkle-covered cake for a hat

Red licorice eyebrows

Chocolate chip and yellow candy-covered chocolate eyes

Candied cherry nose

Red licorice mouth

Licorice chin strap and mustache

RACOON

Small cupcake cut in half with pieces of chocolate buttons for ears

Chocolate chip and yellow candy-covered chocolate eyes

Red candy-covered chocolate nose

Chocolate sprinkle fur

White chocolate button and licorice nose

ELEPHANT

Pink fondant circles on small cupcakes for ears

Red candy-covered chocolate

White chocolate chip tusks

Pink fondant trunk curled up on a small cupcake

TEDDY BEAR

Chocolate button ears

White chocolate chip and licorice eyes

Chocolate sprinkle-covered snout

DOG

Chocolate chip eyes

Licorice nose

Chocolate sprinkle whiskers

Red candy-covered chocolate tongue

Chocolate chip eyes

33

A Rich Chocolate Cake

No birthday or party is complete without a surprise cake – so here's how to make a wonderful chocolate cake that tastes delicious. Look on the next four pages to find out how to cut up, frost and decorate the cake to make an amazing chocolate dinosaur that you will never forget!

You will need

1/2 cup (1 stick) softened butter

1 cup milk

2 eggs

1 tablespoon lemon juice

COOK'S TOOLS

Wire rack

Mixing bowl

Wax paper

9¹/₂ in. springform pan†

Pencil

Scissors

Measuring cup

Strainer

Spoon

Wooden spoon

What to do

1 Set the oven to 350°F.* Grease and flour the pan. Trace around the cake pan on wax paper. Cut out the circle and put it in the pan.

2 Stir the lemon juice into the milk. Put the butter and half the sugar into the mixing bowl and beat together until fluffy.

†Make sure the pan is at least 2¹/₂ in. deep.

* Make sure an adult is there to help.

*1¹/4 cups
granulated sugar*

1 teaspoon baking soda

*³/4 cup
cocoa powder*

1¹/4 cups white flour

3 Beat the eggs into the mixture one at a time. Stir in the rest of the sugar. Sift the flour, soda and cocoa together into a small bowl.

4 Beat in half the milk and fold in half the dry ingredients. Add the rest of the milk and then the dry ingredients. Mix until smooth.

5 Pour batter into pan and bake for almost 1 hour. Cool in pan for 15 minutes. Remove from pan, take off paper and cool on wire rack.

SHAPING THE DINOSAUR

Cut the cake into the pieces shown below with a sharp knife.* Be careful to make your cuts in the right places. If you make a mistake, stick the cake back together with some of the buttercream frosting shown on pages 30 to 31 and start again. Opposite, you can see how to make the dinosaur's scales and spikes from either marzipan, or ¾ cup firmly packed prepared fondant icing.†

Body

Leg   Leg

Spare pieces of cake that you can eat now!

Tail

Head

Neck

† Ready-made fondant may be ordered from Maid of Scandinavia, 32-44 Raleigh Avenue, Minneapolis, MN 55416. Phone 800-328-6722

* Ask an adult to help you with this.

You will need

2 tablespoons egg, slightly beaten[†]

1 cup finely ground almonds

¹/₄ teaspoon green food coloring

³/₄ cup confectioners' sugar

Making marzipan

Put the sugar and almonds in the mixing bowl and stir them together. Add the egg and mix to form a firm paste.

Marzipan scales

Divide the marzipan in half and mix the green coloring into one half. Roll it into balls and squash them flat. Makes about 30.

Marzipan spikes

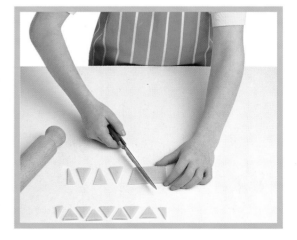

Dust the surface and rolling pin with confectioners' sugar. Roll the marzipan until it is ¹/₈ inch thick. Cut out 12 small and 6 big spikes.*

[†]Egg substitute can be used in place of raw egg if salmonella poisoning is a concern.

37

A DELICIOUS DINOSAUR

And here is the finished dinosaur! Find out how to make buttercream frosting on pages 30 to 31. You will need to triple the ingredients shown and add a few drops of green food coloring.

You will need

1 white chocolate button

1 chocolate chip

Marzipan spikes (see page 37)

Marzipan scales (see page 37)

White chocolate chips

Green buttercream frosting (see pages 30 to 31)

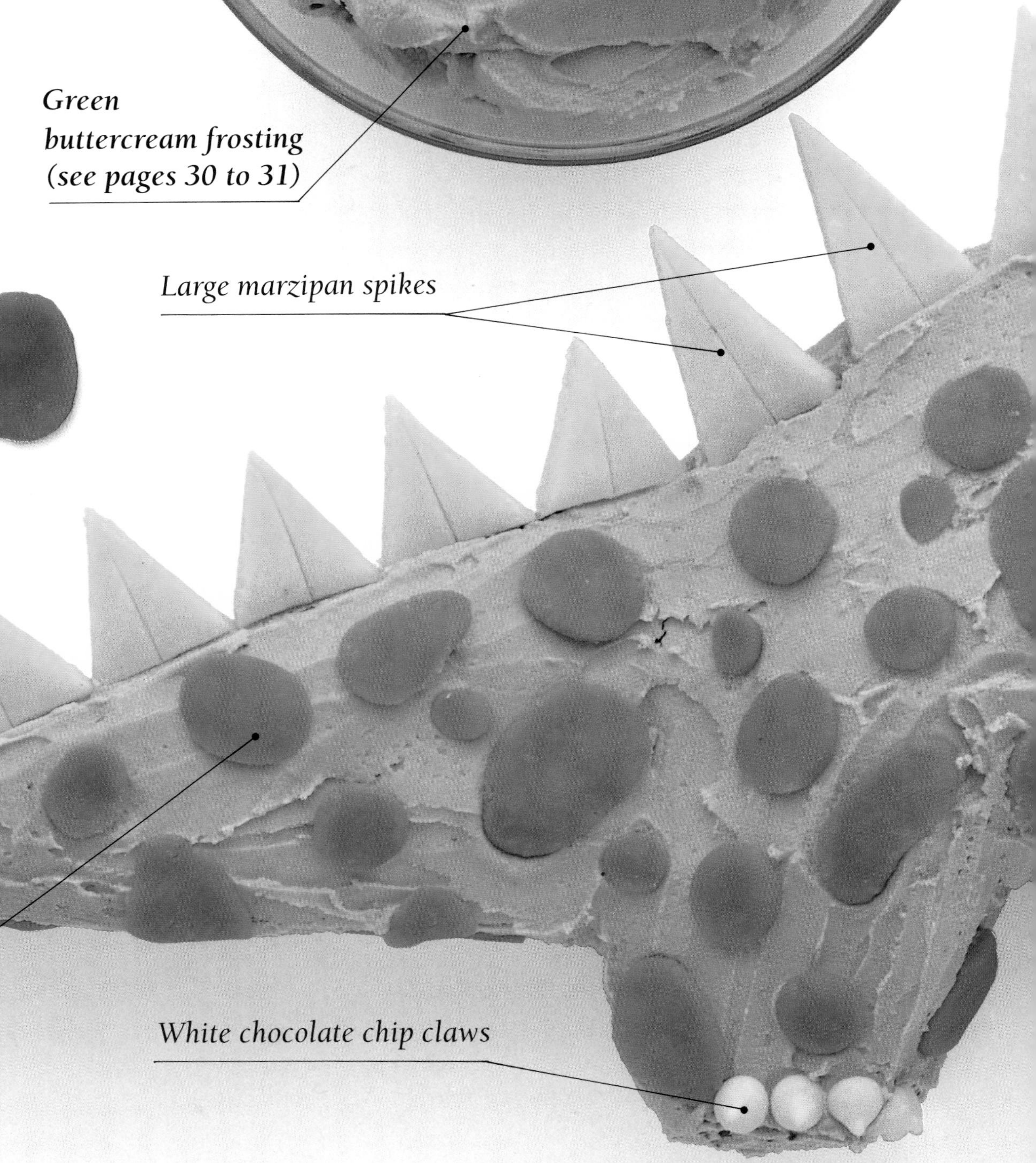

Large marzipan spikes

Marzipan scale

White chocolate chip claws

Decorating the cake

1 Put the cake on the board you will be serving it on. Turn the head on its side and then cut out the dinosaur's jaw.*

2 Use half the frosting to frost the top and sides of each section of cake. Stick the sections together with more frosting.

3 Smooth the rest of the frosting over the whole cake. Decorate the cake with marzipan shapes and chocolate drops, as shown.

The finished cake

Small marzipan spikes

Eye made of a white chocolate button with a chocolate chip on top

White chocolate chip teeth

*Ask an adult to help you with any cutting.

39

PEANUT BUTTER COOKIES

These mouth-watering cookies are very quick and easy to make. Crunchy peanut butter makes the cookies very nutty, but use smooth peanut butter if you prefer it. Bake the cookies for 15 minutes if you like them soft in the middle, or for 20 to 25 minutes if you like them crisp. Store the cookies in an airtight container to keep them fresh.

You will need

3/4 cup firmly packed light brown sugar

1 egg

1/2 cup crunchy peanut butter

1/2 cup (1 stick) softened butter

1 cup self-rising flour

COOK'S TOOLS

2 teaspoons

Spatula (not shown)

Wooden spoon

Mixing bowl

Wire rack

Knife

Greased cookie sheet

What to do

1 Ask an adult to help you. Set the oven to 350°F. Cut up the butter in a bowl and add the sugar. Cream them together until fluffy.

2 Add the peanut butter, flour and egg and beat everything together with the wooden spoon until the dough is smooth.

3 Put teaspoonfuls of dough on a cookie sheet. Bake them for 15 to 25 minutes.* Put them on a wire rack to cool using the spatula.

The finished cookies

*See the introduction to this recipe.

41

Simple Shortbread

Two-tone shortbread biscuits are great fun to make and eat. On this page you can see everything you will need to make plain and chocolate shortbread dough. The ingredients shown below make enough shortbread for eight owl's eyes, eight lollipops and twelve window cookies. Look on the next page to find out how to make each cookie and to see the finished results.

You will need

1/2 cup (1 stick) softened butter

COOK'S TOOLS

Pastry brush

Sharp knife

2 greased cookie sheets

Rolling pin

Mixing bowl

Wooden spoon

Wire rack

Spatula

Popsicle sticks

Strainer

1/3 cup granulated suga

Scant 1/3 cup cocoa powder

8 almonds

1 cup white flour

For chocolate shortbread

½ cup (1 stick) softened butter

⅓ cup granulated sugar

1 scant cup white flour

3 tablespoons milk

Making plain shortbread

1 Make sure an adult is there to help. Set the oven to 350°F. Sift 1 cup flour into the mixing bowl. Stir in ⅓ cup sugar.

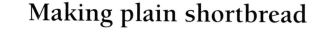

2 Add 1 stick butter, cut up. Rub the flour, sugar and butter together with your fingertips until the mixture is like breadcrumbs.

3 Add a tablespoonful of milk to the mixture. Mix everything together with your hands to form a ball of dough.

Making chocolate shortbread

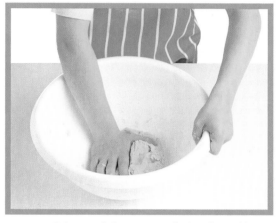

1 Sift together 1 scant cup flour and the cocoa powder. Make the chocolate dough in the same way as the plain dough.

2 Divide each ball of dough into three equal pieces. You will need one plain and one chocolate piece to make each type of cookie.

BISCUIT BAZAAR

Owl's eyes

1 Roll a piece of each type of dough into a square 6 inches by 6 inches. Brush the top of each square with milk.

2 Put one square on top of another and roll them up together. Then cut the roll into 16 slices, as shown.*

3 Stick two slices together with milk to make each cookie. Put the cookies on a cookie sheet. Add an almond beak to each one.

Lollipops

1 Roll the chocolate dough into a square 4 inches by 4 inches. Make the plain dough into a roll 4 inches long with your hands.

2 Brush the chocolate square with milk and wrap it around the plain roll. Press the edges of the chocolate dough together.

3 Cut the roll into eight slices.* Put the slices on the cookie sheet and push a popsicle stick into the middle of each one.

Windows

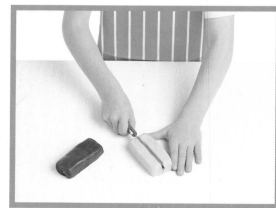

1 Shape the two kinds of dough into rectangles 1½ inches by 3½ inches with your hands. Cut them in half lengthwise.

2 Stick two strips of plain and chocolate dough together with milk. Stick the other two strips on top of them, as shown.

3 Cut the block of dough strips into 12 square slices with a sharp knife.* Put the slices on a cookie sheet.

*Ask an adult to help you with any cutting.

Baking the cookies

4 Bake the cookies in the center of the oven for 15 to 20 minutes until they are a pale gold color. The lollipop cookies are thicker and will take slightly longer to cook.

When the cookies are done, carefully move them from the cookie sheets with a spatula and put on a wire rack to cool.

Storing your cookies

Cookies get soggy if they are left out for too long. Store them in an airtight container to keep them fresh and crunchy.

The finished cookies

OWL'S
EYES

LOLLIPOPS

WINDOWS

CHOCOLATE BROWNIES

Chocolate brownies are a favorite family treat. They are crisp on the outside but wonderfully soft and chewy inside. Below are all the ingredients you need to make dark-chocolate-and-walnut brownies. On the next page you will find the finished brownie squares.

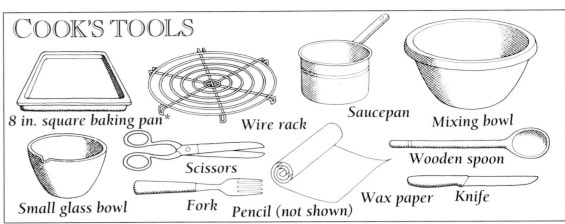
You will need

2 oz semisweet chocolate

5 tablespoons butter

What to do

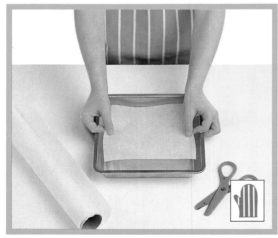

1 Set oven to 350°F. Trace around the baking pan on the wax paper. Cut out the square and put in the bottom of the prepared pan.*

2 Heat some water in the saucepan until it just starts to bubble. Put the butter in the small glass bowl and cut it up.

3 Break up the chocolate into the bowl and place it over the pan as shown. Stir the chocolate and butter together until melted.†

46

* Ask an adult to help you.   †Set aside to cool a bit.

1/2 cup chopped walnuts

2 eggs

3/4 cup light brown sugar, packed

1/2 cup self-rising flour

4 Break the eggs into the mixing bowl and beat with a fork. Add the flour, walnuts and sugar and mix with the wooden spoon.

5 Pour the melted chocolate and butter into the mixture in the bowl and beat them hard until the batter is smooth.

6 Pour the batter into the baking pan and bake for 30 to 35 minutes. Let it cool in the pan and then cut it into squares.

A Brownie Pack

Brownies can be made with any kind of chocolate or nut. Try using white or milk chocolate instead of semi-sweet and using other sorts of nuts – such as hazelnuts, peanuts or almonds – instead of walnuts.

The finished brownies